NEW STRUNG
BOW

NEW STRUNG BOW

A COLLECTION OF POEMS BY
TWENTY-NINE UNDERGRADUATES
AT SARAH LAWRENCE COLLEGE

FOREWORD

BY

LEE WILSON DODD

New York
E. P. DUTTON & COMPANY, INC.

NEW STRUNG BOW

Printed in U. S. A.

FIRST EDITION

To

KATHARINE LIDDELL

FOREWORD

The undergraduate editors of this collection of verse written by undergraduates of Sarah Lawrence College have asked me to write for them a few words of introduction. I am delighted to do so, for I think this small anthology a very gallant and significant undergraduate enterprise. It is entirely an undergraduate enterprise. It was not suggested to the students concerned in it. They conceived the idea themselves and have carried it through themselves to its present happy conclusion. The publishers of this book accepted it on its merits, and it is offered by them to the public as worthy of serious consideration.

Sarah Lawrence is a college devoted to progressive education. Work in the arts is not treated here as a side issue, something graceful and charming, doubtless, but a little removed from the central interests of life. Here, on the contrary, creative activity in the arts is fostered and seems to take its place as something normal and desirable in any well-rounded scheme of human values. In such an environment the writing of verse can no longer be considered, as it is too often considered elsewhere, a somewhat eccentric and possibly even a deleterious occupation.

Poetry has been called the Cinderella of the arts; but poetry, at Sarah Lawrence, is anything but a neglected Cinderella—she is rather the happy Cinderella who knows herself beloved. Nobody snubs her. Indeed, if she were anyone but Cinderella, who is by definition unspoilable, she might even run some little danger of being spoiled. She has here, by the way, two or three Fairy Godmothers, at least; and to one of them, Miss Liddell, this book has been dedicated by her grateful students.

There is one member of the English Department, the rhymer writing these prosaic lines, who is, I confess, a little dazed by this publication! Nothing so splendid ever happened to him or his fellows in their undergraduate days. But other times, other publishers—and perhaps too, alas, other undergraduates!

For, at their best, these undergraduates are able to write directly, poignantly, sincerely, with a minimum of false flourish and borrowed sentiment, if not always, nor often, with the command of a fully matured technique. The promise, however, is apparent. And meanwhile, there are at least two poems in this anthology (but let their names remain my secret) of which I am distinctly jealous; I should like so very much to be able to feel that I might have written them myself.

LEE WILSON DODD.

ACKNOWLEDGMENTS

The thanks of the editors are due to the publishers of *The Keynote*, the *Magpie*, the *Blue Bowl*, the *Georgia Anthology*, the *Washingtonian, Interludes, The Carillian, Embryo*, the *Detroit Saturday Night*, and *Harvest & Other Poems* for permission to reprint poems which have previously appeared in their columns.

CONTENTS

CONTENTS

CONTENTS

CONTENTS

CONTENTS

NEW STRUNG
BOW

Changes

I loved you.
Yes—I did,
And I remember
How we stood
On that windy hill,
And watched the sea
Like corduroy below.

And I remember
How the wind blew papers
And whistled—
And how we walked briskly
Down the quaint old street
To wharves.

That day we watched great angry gulls
Dip and soar
And heard them scream.
They were flashing in the sun.
We sat dangling our feet
Above the water.
We laughed
And looked up at the sky.
We loved the sea.

It seems so strange
That now
You should be
Only a friend to me.
It used to be our minds and hearts
That met—so beautifully.

But hearts—
Hearts are funny things.
They change so suddenly,
So quietly.
And minds love on
Indifferently.
It's strange to me.

Mary Elizabeth Acker

Death

Death took her:
A dear little lady.
I didn't feel as though
Death
Were in that house.

Flowers were there
On the coffin:
Bright flowers,
Light flowers,
Sunlit flowers.

And above these,
A picture
Rich in blue-green—
A Puvis de Chavannes.

My gaze was there:
I knew her spirit
Free—now—
In such Elysian Fields must be—
With such far horizons.

Mary Elizabeth Acker

Laughter of the Gods

There is low laughter,
   Sweet and musical
Like a stream.
   There is the strained laughter
From sorrow.
   There is scornful, proud laughter;
There is child laughter,
   And the laughter of love.
There is something else;
   I have heard it before—
The deep, divine laughter
   Of the gods.
Amused by our struggling world,
   They revel in our follies.
But we are their own work—
   The laugh is on them.

Mary Elizabeth Acker

Leaf

I held out my hand to catch a leaf,
That was falling down to the ground;
But the leaf twirled by my empty hand—
And I heard a laughing sound.

What was it then that laughed?
I looked up to the ancient tree—
I saw its gnarled and twisted boughs,
And saw that they laughed at me.

I wondered then if that tree were a tree—
And I wondered—until I knew—
That it was no tree—but heedless Fate,
And the little leaf—was you!

Mary Elizabeth Acker

Sal

I reckon I'se jes' no 'count a-tall—
Cain't do nothin' no mo' but set an' dream.
W'en Sal war hyer, she uster call
Me to fetch her wood an' water. Seem
Lak ain't never nothin' to do now
Since Sal done gone an' daid he'se'f.
'Members 'way back yander how
Sal'd put her sewin' on tha she'f,
An' set me down befo' tha fier,
An' hol' ma haid an' pray,
An' all time she so tiahed
Hu'se'f f'um wukin' all day.

Preacher say when he done be'd Sal,
"Levawga, don't you weep no mo'
'Cause you done los' yo' gal—
Look whut de Lawd got!" So
I reckons how de Lawd am satisfied.
He sho' got a good woman,
W'en he took Sal f'um ma side.
I finks 'er her a-swimmin'
'Roun' in them pink sunset skies,
All fat again an' happy,
An' a spawkle in her eyes;

She got her maw an' pappy
Up yander, so I reckons I
Gits usta Sal bein' gone,
T'wel comes dc time fo' my
Hearin' ole Gab'el blow he' hawn.

Mary Beane

In Praise of Ananias

"I'll live for truth," you calmly said.
    Your eyes were grey and clear.
"Deceit has roots in cowardice,
    Small lies arise from fear."

Your face was candid as you sought
    Pale truth through meditation;
Your lips were frank, you clearly felt
    My decent admiration.

Truth is indeed a noble thing,
    But apt to make you brittle.
Do think what charm you'd have, my dear,
    If you would lie a little.

Sarah Collie

Silver Night

Out of blue-black depths
Into blue-black eternity
An old man wanders the sky tonight.

Scornful of the winds,
Disdaining the stars,
He points with old silver fingers
At man meddling with emotions.

Sarah Collie

Trees

Half the year from windy air,
Roots are hidden—cold and bare.
But in winter, from earth's darkness,
They come to see the world's renown—
In gigantic forms of boldness
Stand in profile upside down.

Margaret Hill Collins

Why Do You Doubt?

Why do you doubt
Because you cannot see
The force that moves the world?
You say you have no faith
In things you cannot hear
Or see or feel.

But do you doubt your friend?
You know him but in part:
His voice—the words he says;
His hands—the things he does;
His face—the way he looks.
All these are but the outer signs
Of him you cannot see.
Yet do you doubt
That he is there?

Why then doubt God,
Whose outward signs
Are everywhere?

Margaret Hill Collins

Mood

A rough stone wall;
Tall trees, black against a cloud-swept sky;
A wind bending low the grasses;
And bright goldenrod in the field:
This I glimpsed in passing,
And grew suddenly lonely.
I hurried on.
But all day
I knew the wind was still
Bowing down the goldenrod.

Laura Norton Collord

Study in Black and White

Blackness, crystallized,
And stretching upward to the night,
Dropped on the fields and through the air.
Frozen darkness wrapt itself
Around the angles of the roofs,
And found the corners of the valleys—
Blowing over the hills—drowning the light of voices.
Blackness that reached
Cold, sharp and deep, upward and beyond.

But blackness suddenly was shattered
By whiteness falling through its depths;
Silent lightness searching for the corners of the valleys,
And touching gently
The tops of sleeping hills.
Cool foam wrapped the little needles of the pines.
Roofs were warmed.
The night itself rested more gently on the earth
When it was touched
By snow.

Laura Norton Collord

Pity

If I should see white bones
Strewn on the ground,
Upturned from their black graves
By careless spades,
I should not turn away,
But pick them up,
And gently put them back
Into the earth.

Marcia Conger

Filling Cracks

"But—" said I, looking at him,
"Do you not weary of a life
 Like this?"
 From the top rung of a paint-daubed ladder,
 As he stood on his heels
 Smearing putty into a ceiling crack,
 He looked at me—
 An old man in the face—
 Wrinkled—tough skinned—a man well on,
 A little stooped in the shoulders,
 A little saggy underneath the chin.
"Well," he said, as he filled the last crack,
"There could be worse things
 Than drawin' wages for an eight-hour job
 Of fillin' cracks and paintin' walls—
 A feller gets so's he can do them things
 And think of somethin' diffrunt if he wants . . ."
 He got off the ladder,
 Squinted a faded eye up at the finished work,
 Took several speculative puffs,
 Smiled oddly at me,
 Leaned on a wall and lit his pipe,
 Shoved the ladder down a few yards.

                                        Victoria Cranford

Foggy Tonight

"Foggy tonight," someone says,
Dropping a damp coat on a chair.
Foggy? Not that—
A veil across the sky
Hiding the tear-bright stars from sight,
And calming the noise-worn world;
Giving the crowded houses a short separate life;
Lending the peace of a brief solitude
To the tall wearied-with-people trees;
Letting the trade-torn pavements
Rest in temporary peace;
And cooling with an infinite compassion
All the broken thoughts of the sad exiles
God has sentenced to this world.
"Foggy tonight," someone says,
Dropping a damp coat on a chair.

Victoria Cranford

Jephthah's Soliloquy

My life is sad—
  The night reproaches me.
The stars are out above the low camp-fire,
  The life within the woods surrounds me,
And my sleeping comrades
  Leave me solitary and alone.

Born in brief love,
  I was forgotten in the afterfire,
And hated
  By the brothers of a lawful union.
When my father died,
  They threw me out with curses and with kicks
And violent words,
  And left me as an outlaw
To retrail my life,
  And live with murderers.

Once pride and exaltation were in me—
  A poet's passion for the beautiful.
When I was young
  I would be fired at the sight of rising sun upon the sea,
And filled with hotness
  At the sight of a small fawn
Mute and reflected in a pool.
  I did not care to kill—

35

I watched with sadness and with love.
   And I would ache because a birch
Was straight and slim and bare.
   Spring cut me with its clean sweet happiness,
And wind along a tall-grassed hill meant agony.

Now all these things are gone.
   I kill to live.
I make as comrades, outlaws—like myself—
   Who are of strange and distant lands,
And banished thence for crimes
   I never knew existed,
Till I was thrown here like a branded slave.

Night fires, and red embers,
   Hot winds, the storm of rain,
The pant of fear, of hate, of sin,
   Are now my lot.
And I am hated and abhorred by all
   Save these that sprawl in sleep beside me—
And I am solitary in surrounding loneliness.

Victoria Cranford

Protest

It is time Christ came again.
   We who were partly tamed
Are wild once more,
   And have been for a thousand years.
A wildbeast keeper does not leave,
   But stays
To drive the savage into conqueredness.
   He does not logic.
"Now that I have shown the way,
   The beast must follow of a self-accord.
The memory of my teachings will endure,
   And these few I have trained more fully
Will complete the education of the other beasts."
   Nor does he do this thing,
To leave bewildered in a hygienic state
   The beasts,
Avowing that the uses of the wired cage
   Are self-apparent to the bornbred of the wood.
He stays.
But Christ forsook us—
   Left the pupils, and a section of a strange book called
      the Bible;
And the world fell unintelligent, and brow-perplexed,
   Into discussion, war, and crime.
True, though to fight through fog to surety
   Makes character, and gold of alchemies . . .

Can beasts that cower in the storm,
   And civil-prey,
Be thought to know that through the bramble-briar
   Full reason lies?
Christ's words are left us,
   But we do not understand.
Perhaps—some do,
   But they can not interpret to the rest.
The beast can never be the total master.
It is time Christ came again.
   He did not stay enough;
And we are savage who have makings to be men,
   And we are eye-closed,
Mute,
   And packed of fear.

Victoria Cranford

When Spring Is Come

When spring is come,
And this now silent stream
Begins to sound its song beneath the bridges
And along the land,
And this now frozen ground is hard no more;
And when the air is vibrant
With the feel of new grass
And new leaves—
Of flowers just begun to grow,
And of warm rain upon warm earth—
And when the sky is warmly blue . . .
Oh, will the voices of young children playing,
Laughing, fighting for the privilege
To be the first in some new game,
And calling to each other
In the deepening dusk,
Hold more unthinking joy of life within the
        echoes' noise
And be more carefree;
And will the sight of them,
So young, and eager, and so happy,
Be more to watch,
Be more to see and smile about,

Be more for thankfulness that there are children
Who can sing and laugh,
And make so much dear loudness in the silence
    of an afternoon—
Than now?

Victoria Cranford

Moonlight

Moonlight?
Perhaps it is the whiteness
Of souls and spirits
Kneeling for a while upon the earth.

Dorothy Desbon

November

November does not care.
She looses the pins that bind her hair,
Shrugs her shoulder and sighs,
And turns to passive sleep.

Dorothy Deshon

Thank God for Noise

Thank God for noise,
For to be still too long
Is to hear the hollow foot-steps of
        things eternal
Moving silently by
On the other side
Of the great divide.

Dorothy Deshon

Today I Felt Like God

Today I felt like God
When I saw, across the street,
Two people meet,
And pass by—each on his way,
Following his destiny.

Dorothy Deshon

To Take Away the Veil of Beauty

To take away the veil of beauty
Is to find beauty yet there,
As the leaves fall from the trees,
Revealing the tendrils of branches.

Dorothy Deshon

Why Am I Thus?

Why am I thus,
A bit of thistle-down
Blowing about?
Neither friend nor lover
Can keep me near;
And if so,
But for a little while.
The wind is in my ear,
The woods are deep.
A voice calls
At each road's turn.
Something rises
With each wave,
And then lies
Hidden in the foam.
I follow, seeking,
But it flies beyond,
And I am left alone,
Far from those I love,
No nearer to the call.
Then suddenly I know
I am not thistle-down;

For where I have met
Friend and lover,
I have felt joy and pain,
And I am held by these.

Dorothy Deshon

Francesca and Paolo

Francesca, moving
Like a wisp of languid music,
Came into the deep green of the evening garden
Where great flowers,
Limp with perfume and deliciously colored,
Posed in groups.
And a mulberry tree,
Twisted with a thousand years of growing,
Writhed its great aching limbs.
Beside twin pools
Of shallow waters,
That were like blind eyes,
Francesca paused
And felt Paolo come to her side
Silently.
She felt his dusky skin
And long, slow gestures—
The droop of eyelids
She adored.
And she turned.
As their eyes met,
Deep pools of silent feeling
Came bubbling out
In laughter—
Laughter that swirled and bounced
And stumbled through the garden,

While their eyes clung together
And sobbed.
They sat on a stone bench,
And Paolo read from a limp book
In a low, limp voice.

The shadows were like negro crooning;
And the sound of the fountain,
The foolish pattering of tears—
The pattering of a stone mouth
Pouring its tiny strand of water
Onto stone.
Above the terrace
The still statue of a virgin,
Stretching its paralyzed arms upward,
Caught a dull reflection of the evening,
And became for a moment
The lovely thing that its creator
Had failed in.
Paolo's voice read on.
The garden faded into blue.
Francesca
Felt a slow ache
Flow through her veins,
Thoughts came
And went too fast to cling to
In a brain
Worn to the nerves
With thinking.
Paolo's voice grew slower—
Faltered—stopped;

And in the pause
Francesca lived so long
The ancient mulberry tree
Seemed to her
A child.
Then like a great wave
The swaying beauty of the garden
Closed them in . . .

Nancy Dougherty

High on Cool Grey Cliffs

High on cool grey cliffs
I'm going to build my house.
It's only going to have
One door,
A great huge oaken one,
High and wide.
It must be high enough
And wide enough
To take the place of all the other doors.
If I should have a furnace man
(Of course I really won't)
He would bring the ashes and the rubbish
Out the door:
I could watch his bent old back
Toiling down the rocky path,
Around the turns,
Until the golden sand
Comes up to meet his feet.
But of course I won't have rubbish
In my house.
If I have visitors
I'll watch them trip across the sand;
I'll see them come and go
Behind the rocks,

Till they come in the door
The furnace man would use.
(Only if they're visitors, they won't know that.)
But then—
I don't think I'll have visitors
In my house;
Because,
If I had a house,
Built high on cool grey cliffs,
If it only had one door,
A great huge oaken one,
High and wide,
High enough and wide enough
To take the place of all the other doors,
The visitors might copy it,
And then
I think
I might not love it any more.

Helen Muir Duffield

Epitaph

I was the son of Ebenezer and Eulalia Ferguson.
I lived in Plainfield, Mass.
They sent me to school.
But I suspected I was a genius,
And didn't choose to learn.
Why?
Geniuses can get along without all that,
Can't they?
But they couldn't understand.
Well, I was a waiter—
In Judy's Ice-Cream Eating-Palace.
But my spirit was standing on a mountain peak, looking
    at a sunset,
And I dropped the tray.
I was sorry—
But they couldn't understand.
Then I went to sea.
And they put me in the engine-room
To grease those roaring wheels and pistons.
But you know how I hated grease.
I told them so—
Yet I let an axle burn out,
And they couldn't understand.
So I went to war.
Yes, I left my lavender clouds behind me this time.
And they put me by the arsenal door

To wait and watch.
And I watched—
Till my eyes fell shut.
And I waited—
Till my knees gave in.
And the clouds came back.
I saw only sunsets,
Then black.
And then they understood.
And told me so—
At sunrise.
So here I am.
Perhaps they were right, after all.

Sally Dunning

Truant

The wind has called—
There must be no delay—
And you will find me gone
When it is day.

The restless night
Has spoken; I must go
Where only high, cold stars
Can ever know.

The trees are silent.
You may search the grass,
And not a broken blade
Tell where I pass.

And you will grieve
For many, many years.
(May I come back sometime—
To see your tears?)

Sally Dunning

Poem

I have tuned my heart to the wind tonight
As a singer's voice to the key.
My soul is out with the wind tonight;
It is wild and strangely free.
I have sung with the mellow star-chimes
And chanted with the moon.
My voice is high with the wind tonight—
It sings no earthly tune.

Mary Eiseman

Concert

I am a reed
Blown by music
Into tremors.
Shaken by a wind
Of notes,
That rips my fiber
And bends me to a stream.
I lie
Submerged in a flood
Of blent tones,
Drowned by melody and chords.

Nancy Flowers

Defeat

She stood
In the crowd
With startled eyes,
A faun;
A flute among cymbals;
With many people
Alone.
Invaded by noise,
She turned,
Aloof but vanquished,
And with tattered banners
Was gone.

Nancy Flowers

Discovery

In an
Ice-cream fountain
Among bottles,
Oranges,
And fancy cake,
I saw him,
His white hair
Reflected
On the polished marble
Of the stand,
Watching
His sleek sons
Move on cat-like feet,
Their trained hands
Infallible in mixing drinks.
He nodded,
And rested
His face
In two palms.
He was not there.
In his eyes
I had seen
A crooked olive tree,
And a patch
Of blue
Italian sky.

Nancy Flowers

59

Late Summer

The lake, ruffled into a million ripples,
Is blue and silver,
Purple where the fishes dart.
A row of birches is shaken into music
Tinkling like glass bells
In the wind.
The sun pours gold upon the water,
Extravagant.
Even lily pads, impoverished green,
Lie burnished in a hoarded light.
Little minnows swish molten tails,
Oblivious.

Nancy Flowers

Let It Be So

I would be tranquil,
Infinitely so,
Floating like a water lily
Upon the surface of my environment.
Then no one could see the long muddy tendrils
Clinging desperately to the changeless bottom of life.

Nancy Flowers

Mute

My thoughts are surging behind
Sealed lips, mute.
Were it not so, my words would be
As blue flowers strewn in the wind,
Remote and delicate,
Forgetful, in their cool simplicity,
Of fragrance.
My words would be as the acid
Tones of bees, sharp and shallow,
Drifting in clamorous procession
Up a dull blue sky—
My words never to be born,
Never to die.

Nancy Flowers

Regret

Today
Has slipped
Like a silver fish
Through the net
Of my consciousness.
I regret
Not having caught
Its elusiveness
Or held the brilliance
Of its scales.

Nancy Flowers

Unicorns

They prance
At night,
Little unicorns,
Across my mind.
Their silver hoofs
Beat down
The valleys
Of my eyes,
Tossing their horns
In a forest
Of hair.
They stamp
A rhythmic,
Noisy fugue,
That jars
My nerves,
And splits
My head.
They pound
My thoughts,
And paw
My dreams,
Then leave
Me bruised,
And void
Of song.

Nancy Flowers

A Visitor

He came to our house once, I believe—
He brought two chairs he had been caning for us.
My mother called him an artist.
His hands reminded me of shifting reeds by a river bank.
He spoke of foreign things:
Junks with lacquered sails;
Hyacinths floating in blue porcelain bowls.
His eyes were restless as the swaying branches of lilacs.
I wonder what he was thinking about
As he thumbed over the pages of that old copy of Verlaine,
While mother stood holding his money—waiting for him.

Nancy Flowers

Round

Round. That is your mind.
    Nothing simpler. Round.
You get up in the morning and start it off on its circle.
It goes all day, and when night comes back again
    It is where it was the night before.
Round. That is your mind.

Margaret Gause

Suggestion

Why tear your hands on the thorns of that rose?
If you sit here in the sun, beside the young birch,
You can see it just as well.

Margaret Gause

Among Falling Leaves

By the side of a little brown country road,
In the fall, when the leaves were turning,
And were even now dropping from the trees
Like bright feathers twisting and burning,
An old woman walked midst the shadows and light,
And the warm, glowing afternoon sun
Touched her gray hair to gold with its peaceful hands,
While the bright leaves fell, one by one.

Jean C. Gibbons

For H. P.

They said I should forget you.
I, the fish in the twisting net
Loving the mighty ocean—
How could I forget?

And have the stars
A less tormenting light
Because they can't be seen by day,
And can't be touched by night?

Eleanor Green

New Strung Bow

There is an eagerness in youth, that fears
To choose one path to follow all its days,
Uncertain of its curves. The silent tears
Fall salted on the heart. A thousand ways
Lift beckoning fingers. Fearfully, youth weighs
Each ounce of this and that; failing to find
The perfect balance in any one, obeys
Each summons for a little while—not blind
To unity but leaving awful choice behind.

And later, should we choose, we see no smile
On welcoming face. How sad, the heart of man,
To laugh and jest, and stay a little while,
And then go singing with the caravan
Of muted throats, never to learn the plan
Of what we strive and suffer for—and die,
Tasting no more than when our lives began,
Reaching our questing fingers to the sky,
And finding our hands barren—God, a strange reply!

Barren our hands, yet even more our hearts,
Who sense the peace, but never reach the place.
For as we near the end, swift peace departs,
And we must struggle on, nor glimpse her face,
Who travels as we do—but half a pace
Ahead. I wonder, if we sang our songs
Eternally through life, could we unlace
This net of intricate design—that longs
To snare—and tuck away some peace where peace belongs.

70

There peace belongs where music finds its rest—
Not altogether undisturbed. No soul
That music haunts, but knows the sheltering breast
To feel despair; or like the blind-eyed mole
Would lose the beauty of the light. The bowl
Of fairy water, sometimes called the sea,
Feels no loss when one drop from the whole
Vanishes in the mist. To what degree,
Then, do we win our race, our bounds, eternity?

A soul is not perfected by the touch
Of silk, the glint of gold, the noise of words,
But by the bitterness of tears, and such
A note of gladness as the winter birds
First carol, seeing spring scatter the herds
Of sullen cattle, weary of winter's face.
With songs of sparrow and whippoorwill spring girds
Her singing throat. Why do we ask which race
Is first or best? Black soul and white hold equal place.

Who is to say who fails, and who succeeds?
We stamp our goods with a long-enduring mark
Of worldly wealth, and pray for gold. Who bleeds
Upon the shrouded altar in the dark,
The altar of self-sacrifice? The spark
Of Christ-fire, hidden deep within us, burns
A while, unfed—then paints a whistling arc
Across the aching sky, and there it learns
That the whole from which it sprang is the part for which
    it yearns.

If giving over self should be the way
To learn, what of these darker brothers to
My "sovereign" race, going, bent, away,
Chanting their song—begin, and chant it through,
Hearing no song in answer. As the dew
Strengthens the thirsty plant, so the taste
Of tolerance. But try the other shoe
Upon *this* foot, and we should soon make haste
To cut the binding strings that we'd so tightly laced.

Unknown, how many twisting strings there be!
The pregnant mind, heavy with stirring thought,
Delicate in sensibility,
Like some rare web by elf and fairy wrought,
Hangs in the open winds and soon is caught
In the arms of passing time, and stands aghast
To see the silent years, that it had sought
So eagerly in youth, go swiftly past—
A ship with its enemy's colors flying from the mast.

Scorn, I have looked full many a time
Into your face; been filled with fear to smell
Your breath—as though ten minutes hence, you'd climb
With rotting body back into the spell
Of death—momentarily freed—and Hell
The while, cracking its brittle sides to find
Your shrouded self; death alone can quell
The ardor of scorn's fire, and slowly wind
Him in his arms—deafen, and make him blind.

Where'er Creation gnaws—(the thin-haired youth),
He leaves in every man the self-same mark.
The flesh, new-torn, is open where the tooth
Has sunken deep, dripping blood as dark
As drops of midnight be.—Where to embark?
Which ship—Creation at the mast—to sail?
With which all-eager breath to blow the spark
That burns uncertainly? Hearing the wail
Of many chiselled stones, which statue to unveil?

Who knows which thing to doubt, and which believe?
Since Peter did, once in the Holy Land,
Mistake his choice, this name he must receive:
"Denier!" Men ate Christ's heart from out His hand,
And later, when they spat upon the sand,
Christ smiled, hearing how slow His heart could beat,
Thinking that later they would understand.
And yet today, nine Judases He'd meet,
And there'd be weeping Magdalens about His feet.

If at the hour of dusk I should forget—
With half-closed eyes watching the silent night
Come creeping stealthily—to pay my debt
Of gracious death; if I should lose the sight
And thirst for beauty ere the passing light
Has gone, and only shadows fill the sky,
Death, to mock me then becomes your right.
In life I may have failed, but let me die
With grace—no moaning agony, no final cry!

Eleanor Green

73

Pagan Wonder

I wonder if the gods
That sit on cushioned
Benches in the sky,
And watch the writhing
Of my pagan soul,
Have felt cracked laughter,
Terrible and real,
Strangle in their throats;
If they have felt cold rain
Against their ever-smiling cheeks,
Or gloried in
The early evening stars.
I wonder if far-reaching
Limbs of trees have grappled
With their hearts,
And wrung the tears from out their souls.
And if they have known any one of these,
They are more merciless and cruel
Than they seem now.

Eleanor Green

Pan's Madness

One time I said I flew.
My parents feared,
As though they knew
Already I was queer.

And once I said my ears
Were big—like Pan's.
My parents' fears
Were multiplied by two.

And now—because it only
Makes them sad,
I never say these things aloud—
So now, of course, they think I'm mad.

Eleanor Green

She Fed the Quail

She fed the quail that gathered at the door
In winter time, and stroked the young colt's head,
Or rolled a ball along the kitchen floor
To tease the orphan lamb, that had its bed
Behind the stove, to rollicking about.
She only opened up the faded box
Of baby clothes to shake the wrinkles out,
Or add new sprigs of mignonette and phlox.

She'd wait to hear him call the cows at night,
Counted ten before he closed the gate,
Watched the pattern of his swinging light,
Smoothed the table-cloth when he was late;
But when he laid his head upon her breast,
Her minute sorrow sang itself to rest.

Eleanor Green

This Dusky Child

She enters late; her step is proud—
Aloof. She draws her ermine cloak
Tighter, as to keep the crowd
Away—for there are colored folk.

She does not see this dusky child
With woolen shawl about her throat,
Whose deep brown eyes are sad and wild
As music sings of lands remote.

Eleanor Green

Admission

No, it is not my regret
That I, miserable one,
Live a life in quotations.
It is not my sorrow
That I make my grief
Only a sudden reflection of Shelley's;
My exultation
A faint whimpering after Browning's.

But, oh, for a heart not placid as mine
To tell you
That you are Inheritor of the Ages.

Mary Katherine Hogle

Topping the Weeds

Came I,
Running my swiftest,
Swinging a stick,
Leaving green stalks
Broken and hanging.

Then I,
Falling to the ground,
Heard blood flow,
Felt a heart beat,
Knew my kinship with soil.

Mary Katherine Hogle

The Docks

Ships from far away places;
Water full of oil and old wood;
Huge crates and great barrels;
Yellow dogs, cringing from the seamen;
The long cry of gulls;
Ropes, chains, grease, sails;
The smoke of a trusted pipe;
And the tiny slap of beckoning waves,
Calling men back to the sea.

Carra M. Hutchinson

Leaf Poem

My thoughts are like falling leaves,
More beautiful for the bitterness
Of frosts—
Perhaps they will be gathered
And fill the air with the pungent odor
Of smoke.
Or perhaps the brightness of one
May amuse some child
Till, like a leaf,
It withers and dies.

Carra M. Hutchinson

New Madness

The old moon died.
It staggered blindly across the sky,
Bade farewell to a frightened star,
And sank into the waiting arms
Of the hungry sea.

But
Out of the void
A new moon was born.
And men have forgotten the old moon.
They live only
In a madness of new moons,
And the clinging scents of pear blossoms
Drifting down to the dark earth.

Carra M. Hutchinson

To Be Young

To be young is to tear
The petals off the flower,
Then, weeping, try to put
Them on again.

Elizabeth Hyde

Up and Down

Up and down, up and down,
Over, all over this terrible town.
Up and down—each time I'll go
Just a bit more slow;
And once I hope I'll know
Why it is I go
Up and down, up and down,
Seeking what in this terrible town?
What and where? Up or down?
Which and when in this terrible town?

Elizabeth Hyde

Autobiography

I am a moment—
A singer of jazz,
A dealer in dreams,
A ticker of stocks,
A buzzing
Green fly.

I pass in the streets
Racing and chasing.
I laugh in the wind,
I swish like a rocket,
I burn out,
I die.

Dorothy Kirkpatrick

I Pity Old Ladies

I pity old ladies
With black coats and rabbit fur.
Their cheeks are drawn tight,
And they wear glasses
To help them cross streets
And read hymns
And knit.
I wonder if they have ever stood
On a moon-washed beach,
Curled white by night waves;
Looked into the darkness,
Laughed at it,
Hugged it close;
Stood fearless, with hands clasped high,
Feeling the wind.
I wonder this,
Pitying old ladies
With black coats and rabbit fur.

Dorothy Kirkpatrick

Mamie's Song Over the Wash Tub

Down in th' canefiel's don' you hyeh th' niggas sing?
An' th' steady swishin' music of th' cuttin' sickle's swing?
O, th' juice of th' cane is a-flowin' jest as sweet
As th' voices of th' angels all aroun' th' Jedgment Seat.
 Swing high, niggas.
 No time fo' sleep an' sunnin'.
 Satan might ketch you,
 An' Pay-Day is a-comin'.

Misteh Jay-Bird is a-squawkin' in the big magnolia trees;
The honeysuckle's heavy with th' buzzin' bumble-bees.
Oooo, Lawd,
Winteh is a-comin' with its trouble an' its sorra,
But today th' sun is shinin', an' Pay-Day is temorra.
 Splash that watch
 Hyeh th' banjos strummin'?
 Git behin' me, Satan.
 Pay-Day's a-comin'.

O we'll come from up th' riveh, from th' bayou an' th'
  fiel's
In piled up wooden wagons with creakin', swayin' wheels.
We'll gather like th' Heavenly Host in shiny bright array,
An' I'll buy myself some earrin's on the happy holiday.
 Bright red earrin's.
 Nigga, hyeh th' washboard drummin'.
 Oooo Lawd in Hebe'n,
 Pay-Day is a-comin'!

Florence Laws

87

Perversity

When I was there,
And the quiet waters of the lake lapped in little sounds,
And the sheltering wood
Was green and tall near by,
I often wished for a sweep of surf
And an open view of the sky.
When I am here,
And the night wind moans across the moor,
And the waves roll pounding on the sand;
Oh, to be in a boat on the star-filled lake
With a scent of sweet fern from the land!

Grace McCreary

White Horses

Last night the wind leapt at the trees.
His voice was like the roar of the ocean,
And in my heart I saw the foam-flecked, gray-blue sea.

Poseidon stood in his chariot.
Out floated his mantle of spray.
I saw his white-maned horses rear,
Plunge thunderously down,
Dart proudly up the sands,
Then slink, defeated, back
To try again.

Melicent Makepeace

August

The summer has long spider legs
That curve under me and keep me
Spinning in a dizzy, hot laziness.
I listen across the damp, still dark
To the continually commenting crickets.
The tree outside my window twists a little—
It must be almost morning.
I hear the bare feet of the crab women
Thudding on the pavement.
The moaning roll of wooden cart wheels rumbles in the
    distance,
Comes nearer and grumbles away again.
If I fan with my fingers,
It might make a little wind.
Summer is so still in the dark,
Like an old, old lady
Nodding.

Betty Myers

The Bumpy Iron Back Stairs

The bumpy, iron back stairs
Are like your will—
Thin and regular
And merely useful looking,
Very conventionally useful;
Until I trip over them
And get up with both knees
Bleeding.

Betty Myers

La Mort

When I was little, once I heard it said,
"Men are the greatest who have long lain dead."
And so I threw my soldier's soul away
And let him sleep beneath my plant one day.
But when I brought him back, he had to lie
Out in the sun to let the dampness dry.
And other things that died and went away
Seemed no more great with passing of each day.
"Oh, Life," I mourned, "make it that I shall see
The fame or not that death will bring to me."
And from the wind a curious smell arose—
The dampness drying from my soldier's clothes.

Betty Myers

Sacrilege

I sit in the dazzling splendor of Roxy's.
Little Moor balconies,
Sculptured towers,
Loom brazenly above me.
Thousands of years from now
People will dig them up
And say, "Behold, a temple!"

Betty Myers

To a Delicate Actress

Your grease paint is thick and clumsy,
And those eyelashes are too heavy to be your own.
Your nails are red with artificial fervor.
They are all too heavily empty.
But your hand shook ever so little when he kissed you:
That was light enough to be you.

Betty Myers

When I Stay Out at Night

When I stay out at night,
The latch key waits
Inside the stone vase
Where our boxwood grows.
Oh dreadful, dreadful thought!
If I'm too late,
It may take root;
Returning, I shall see
Thousands of jangling flowers
Awaiting me.

Betty Myers

Me

There are bits of earth in me, I know:
A bit of brown New England sand
From country roads, patterned by the sun through leaves;
A bit of rich black loam from fibrous roots,
Damp and dark beneath the apple trees.
There are bits of clouds too:
Strong, white billows,
Clean and glorious from the Northwest;
And the thousand stupid, aimless scuds
That fill the sky before it rains.

Virginia Riggs

The Clock Goes "Tock"

The clock goes "tock,"
The bird says "peep,"
The breeze says "swish"—
    I'm asleep.

The clock goes "tick,"
The world's a fake,
And life's a problem—
    I'm awake.

Virginia Riggs

Forgetting

I see my elongated reflection
In the metal roundness of the berth above me.
I wish I could look like that—
Long, slim legs—thin face.
My fingers, too,
Like an artist's.
How chubby I am, really.

This feeling so intently scraping
In my stomach.
Not an ill feeling.
I've had it before,
On the roller coaster—
Singing Christmas carols.
Sometimes it's too painful—
As now.
But I love it.

That's why I see my reflection
And count up to fifteen between snores
Across the aisle.
Once it was sixteen.

God! this feeling swells so.
Expectation—suspense.
That's locating it technically.

Outside
A black west streaks by.
Those rapid wheels make it so.
I love the engineer.

Through this darkness
He keeps a throttle pushed in
At the top-speed mark.
Funny how we all look down on engineers—
We social ones.
I don't now.
I wish the window would open.
I could lean out
And wave my admiration.
Silly.

This feeling won't lessen until
Tomorrow,
Seven-fifteen A.M.
If I could only go to sleep.
But I've never felt more awake.

Will she seem surprised
To have me eager?
I wouldn't say, "Darling,"
Or "I've changed so—all about you,"
In letters.

Too obvious—
She'd think I was forcing it.
Besides, I want her to see it tomorrow,
At seven-fifteen A.M.
All at once—

Like a streak of sunlight,
Ever-broadening.

I will just look at her,
Then walk with our arms linked.
She always had to do that all herself—
So wistful.

I'll tell her of the images I've seen
On sunny days
At a dormitory window.
How I remembered her,
One day last summer,
Getting off the street-car.
She had purple iris
And a white fox fur.
She was happy.
I was sitting on the porch.
She waved,
And danced a little step.
"Hello, darling."
"Hello," I said.
But I remembered—
Even in my indifference.

Then again,
When I came home from school
And went up to her room.
She was sitting in her blue chair,
A book on her lap.
There was an apple core and a cracknel

On the window sill.
She looked at me.
There was sunlight at the window.

"Guess I'll go over to Louise's," I said,
And walked out.

I'll tell her why I was so angry
That time when she got home late,
And I'd been wondering
For two hours,
And had read all the accident reports
In the papers,
And telephoned everywhere
She came in
Hoping I would be like that.
"My Lord! You've kept dinner waiting two hours!"
I said.

I'll tell her of books I've read—
"Ambrose Holt and Family—"

How I sobbed
When I finished,
And was afraid of waking my room-mate;
And why I sobbed.
I remember once
When she was reading "Rasputin,"
She told me about it.
"You must read it, Peg."
"I don't like the sound of it," I said.

I was waiting for Scott,
Looking over my shoulder in the mirror.

I'll ask her
How she and Dad met—
If she had loved many others—
How it was having me.
She tried to tell me once.
I was embarrassed.
It made her embarrassed too,
And inconsequential.

I'll sit in her room
While she dresses
For a dinner-dance.
I'll tell her that her dress is becoming,
And discuss the unusualness of the color,
And how remarkable that her hair
Is still so golden.
Once, wistfully,
She said,
"Ann Holman is only two years older than I
And have you noticed how grey her hair is becoming?"
"I haven't noticed it," I said.

I'll sit on her bed at night.
I'll tell her what a marvelous dance it was.
And I'll describe
Dresses,
Music,
And the crowd.
Then I'll take off my shoes
And tell her how my feet ache;
Then, becoming personal,

How Bill Wilcox had asked me
To ride on up the highway
To Horse-Tail Falls;
And how Scott had sworn off drinking.
Once, he gave me his pin;
She saw it on my dresser.
"Peg—what a good-looking pin.
Why, it's a fraternity seal!
Was it Scott, darling?"
She was laughing,
Excited for me,
"He gave it to me last night," I said,
And twisted a dial on the radio.

I'll tell her how they all love her—
Louise, Kat, Scott,
Jean, Guy, Sarah.
She thinks them all splendid,
And I've agreed.

Oh!
She'll know this—
Talking and laughing
And linking of arms!

This swelling, dizzy feeling
Waving all over me
And under me—
Lifting me up—
Up into thinness—

103

But wait a minute!
You damned engineer!
Clang the bell,
Jerk the throttle,
And stop this train,
I keep forgetting
That she is dead.

Margaret Riley

Like Some Great Light

All that in life which is so strange and sweet
Has touched my life with sudden loveliness,
But like the wind on restless winged feet
It speeds on by and leaves this loneliness.
Like some great light, all beauty floods my mind;
It burns, then dims to just a memory,
As though some power had feared to leave behind
These few sweet fragments of reality.
A lovely moment seems so small a thing,
A misty thing all wrapped in ecstasy,
Until it dims and leaves me questioning
Because it takes away a part of me.
May death be just the finding of sublime
And lovely moments linked in ageless time.

Virginia Spiker

9:42 Local

Row on row of shabby heads—
Nodding, jerking, twisting heads—
All with hats, some with glasses,
Bending over *Snappy Stories*,
Peering through the rain-streaked panes.
Drowsy heads like wilted poppies,
Drooping sideways, back and forth,
Jerking upward, down again.

Going some place, going where?
Riding through the slippery night.

See that man with horn-rimmed glasses
Wheezing some and sound asleep?
A horrid little girl with freckles
Pokes him hard, then grins and grins.
A large salubrious woman
Bounces in staccato time,
And shining cherries dangle
About her sand-pail hat.
An old, old woman,
Parched as sun-burnt apricots,
Is seeing things through mist-filled eyes.
I think she dreams of distant youth
Because she looks at me and smiles.
There's *savoir faire* jiggling there
In Persian lamb and diamond rings.
A smile half parts her cerise lips;

106

Her eyes have caught the lustrous glow
Of Broadway nights—
They hint at gay and wicked things.
She quite forgets she jiggles so,
And bounces with the row on row
Of shabby heads.

Going some place, going where?
Riding through the slippery night.

Beside me sits a working man,
Gray as ashes that have stood too long.
His gnarled fingers tightly grasp
A battered lunch box by his side.
He chews and chews in measured time
As if he heard a metronome.

"Tickets, please!" . . . he comes at last.
The unavoidable solemn man
Whose misfit shiny suit
Pronounces him the ticket man.
His black shoes curl at the toes,
Perhaps from swaying back and forth.
He never smiles or stops to talk—
Just "Tickets, please," and punches them,
And jiggles on throughout his life.
But look at me! I'm jiggling too,
Jerking, twisting like the rest.
My head is wobbling just a bit,
And knocks against the drafty pane.
I cannot hold it up, it seems,
My eyes are drooping so.

Odd thoughts are whirling through my head.
Papers rustle, wheels are grinding,
A whistle screeches in the drizzle,
Calling out to startle something—
Something in the rushing darkness.
Through half-closed eyes
I see the glistening, rain-streaked pane,
And just beyond, a blur of lustre light
Singeing all the world with copper fire.
I hear a name . . . the ticket man has called a name
In syllables that flood my sleepy brain
With sudden darts.
A bulbous man blinks stupidly,
And holds the door to let me pass.
I feel the chill of rain drops falling,
And breathe out misty shrouds that float across the dark-
    ness.

A whistle; the train slips off.
Going some place, going where?
Riding through the slippery night.

Virginia Spiker

Arizona Night

Howl of a lonely coyote,
Then silence.
Moon, blood-red,
Leering down upon the plain.
Sage-brush quivering
In cruel night wind.
Cloudless sky
Filled with cold stars
Laughing . . . laughing.
Howl of a lonely coyote.
Again silence.

Narcissa Swift

The Altar

Out of the empty void that bound me
As the earth-shores bind the lake,
A sudden brilliance grew around me,
Ecstatic as the quick intake
Of an artist's breath when he wakes to see
His dream become reality;
And this the dream that entered me:

I was alive, divinely one
With Earth, and Star, and Tree, and Sun;
A vital part of the world, and strong
With inward vision;
                     pagan song
Leapt to my throat; earth seemed to sing,
And this I knew was mental spring.

I stood amazed, and suddenly
Realized another me,
With gaunt feet sandaled, and a hood
That priest-like round me hung. I stood
Before an idol, smooth-browed, cold,
And I was old, profoundly old.

Then turned, and saw upon the hill
An altar standing white and still,
Encircled by ethereal light.
I looked no more to left or right,

But left the out-grown idol. God,
Personified in flame and sod,
Was burning at the altar's fire.
And Love and Spiritual Desire
Like ocean breakers through me surged.

.   .   .   .   .

Then from the darkened wood emerged
That other me, divine and young,
The savage from whom I had sprung
Before the transformation; we,
Two persons of a single name,
Split parts of an entirety,
From warring parts encompassed, came.
Fearing and shunning each other, yet
Over the altar of Art we met.

Susanne Bagley Wallace

Apple Tree

I sought the woods, nor hoped to see
The blossoms of the apple tree;
I sought the woods with hungry eye,
And saw against an April sky
What tore the very heart of me:
O memory of the apple tree!

Susanne Bagley Wallace

Second Avenue Sunset

West windows flame; the wasp-like hum
Of traffic lessens; there has come
To mortal streets immortal pain.
Earth pauses, then revolves again

About three men, who, wrangling, are
Unmindful of an evening star;

About two girls, who, craving bread,
Lurk by dark doors whence lights gleam red;

About one child, who stands apart,
Whistling in a city's heart.

Susanne Bagley Wallace

Harvest

I buried hate beneath a tree,
Upon a jet-black night;
A thousand stars came out to see,
And lent their spectral light;
And suddenly the withered tree
Burst forth in buds of white.

Susanne Bagley Wallace

Prenatal

If I should live, I'll date my birth
From seeing a blind beggar stand
In snow, a spirit-hungry earth
Expressive, through his face and hand.

Susanne Bagley Wallace

Roots

Roots are expansive, wondrous things,
Alive with action as the wings
Of birds. Whoso translates the cry
Of restless gulls across the sky,
May also comprehend the sound
Of roots expanding, underground.

Susanne Bagley Wallace

Two Talk of Gandhi

Small is he, and ugly,
So the papers say;
Once I saw his picture,
And turned my face away.

Bald-headed and pot-bellied;
Thin as any rod, and—

Stop, you fool, I've seen him,
And felt his eyes—Great God!

Therein only spirit
Is, of titan girth.

Small, you think?
                    I think
Of Christ come back to earth.

Susanne Bagley Wallace

Vacation

How rare the man, how happy he,
Who holds a hill in memory;
Who tramps beneath a brain-gleaned sky,
And catches fish in his mind's-eye.
Prince-like his bounty, who can take
To town, within his heart, a lake.

Susanne Bagley Wallace

Vermont Landscape

I like the way the hills roll down,
And up again, beyond the town.

I like the way clean stars shine through
A misty sky of purple hue.

I like the way the village church
Is merged into a clump of birch.

Susanne Bagley Wallace

The Wood

Rich as music was the wood,
And lost in wonder, long I stood.
Suddenly a wild-bird cry
Split the stillness of the sky.
A minute told, and I grew old,
And by my head dim centuries rolled.
How long? Eternity. I stood
For one vast minute in a wood.

Susanne Bagley Wallace